LITTLE DINOSAURS AND EARLY BIRDS

Once there were no birds. That's hard to believe today, when you see birds all around you, soaring and diving, catching insects in midair, pulling up worms.

John Kaufmann explains what fossils tell us about the earliest birds. In clear text and true-to-life pictures he describes how little dinosaurs became birds as millions of years went by and how they began to fly.

LITTLE DINOSAURS AND EARLY BIRDS

Written and illustrated by
John Kaufmann

Thomas Y. Crowell Company
New York

LET'S-READ-AND-FIND-OUT SCIENCE BOOKS

Editors: *DR. ROMA GANS*, Professor Emeritus of Childhood Education, Teachers College, Columbia University
DR. FRANKLYN M. BRANLEY, Astronomer Emeritus and former Chairman of The American Museum–Hayden Planetarium

LIVING THINGS: PLANTS

Corn Is Maize: The Gift of the Indians
Down Come the Leaves
How a Seed Grows
Mushrooms and Molds
Plants in Winter
Roots Are Food Finders
Seeds by Wind and Water
The Sunlit Sea
A Tree Is a Plant
Water Plants
Where Does Your Garden Grow?

LIVING THINGS: ANIMALS, BIRDS, FISH, INSECTS, ETC.

Animals in Winter
Bats in the Dark
Bees and Beelines
Big Tracks, Little Tracks
Birds at Night
Birds Eat and Eat and Eat
Bird Talk
The Blue Whale
Camels: Ships of the Desert
Cockroaches: Here, There, and Everywhere
Corals

Ducks Don't Get Wet
The Eel's Strange Journey
The Emperor Penguins
Fireflies in the Night
Giraffes at Home
Green Grass and White Milk
Green Turtle Mysteries
Hummingbirds in the Garden
Hungry Sharks
It's Nesting Time
Ladybug, Ladybug, Fly Away Home
Little Dinosaurs and Early Birds
The Long-Lost Coelacanth and Other Living Fossils
The March of the Lemmings
My Daddy Longlegs
My Visit to the Dinosaurs
Opossum
Sandpipers
Shells Are Skeletons
Shrimps
Spider Silk
Spring Peepers
Starfish
Twist, Wiggle, and Squirm: A Book About Earthworms
Watch Honeybees with Me

What I Like About Toads
Why Frogs Are Wet

THE HUMAN BODY

A Baby Starts to Grow
Before You Were a Baby
A Drop of Blood
Fat and Skinny
Find Out by Touching
Follow Your Nose
Hear Your Heart
How Many Teeth?
How You Talk
In the Night
Look at Your Eyes*
My Five Senses
My Hands
The Skeleton Inside You
Sleep Is for Everyone
Straight Hair, Curly Hair*
Use Your Brain
What Happens to a Hamburger
Your Skin and Mine*

And other books on AIR, WATER, AND WEATHER; THE EARTH AND ITS COMPOSITION; ASTRONOMY AND SPACE; and MATTER AND ENERGY

* Available in Spanish

Library of Congress Cataloging in Publication Data Kaufmann, John. Little dinosaurs and early birds. SUMMARY: Discusses prehistoric birds and their ancestors and theories on how creatures began to fly. 1. Birds, Fossil—Juv. lit. 2. Dinosauria—Juvenile literature. [1. Birds, Fossil. 2. Dinosaurs] I. Title. QE871.K38 568'.2 75-37575 ISBN 0-690-01110-5

2 3 4 5 6 7 8 9 10

LITTLE DINOSAURS AND EARLY BIRDS

For Aliki

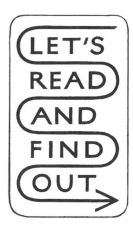

A pigeon sails up into the air. A seagull glides
past with wings spread wide. In the trees, in
fields, and by the seashore, you see many kinds of
birds. It is hard to believe that once there were
no birds at all.

How did birds begin? How long have they lived
on earth? How did they start to fly? For a long
time, no one knew.

1

More than a hundred years ago, scientists found some answers. A fossil was dug up in Germany. It was about one hundred and forty million years old. Some of the bones were broken. The skeleton was twisted out of shape, but most of the bones were still together.

At first, scientists thought it was the skeleton of a small reptile. Many of the other fossils that had been found were skeletons of reptiles. But when they looked at it more carefully, they were surprised. This was different from any other fossil they had ever seen.

The scientists could see that there had been feathers on this creature. And the feathers made the pattern of two wings and a tail.

Archaeopteryx

This was an amazing discovery. They had found the fossil of one of the first birds. It was about the size of a pigeon. They called this early bird Archaeopteryx (Arky-opter-icks), which means "ancient wing." Since then, four more fossils of Archaeopteryx have been found.

Second Fossil
of Archaeopteryx

Ichthyornis

Scientists also found fossils of a more recent bird. This one lived about one hundred million years ago. They called it Ichthyornis (Ick-thee-ornis), which means "fish-bird." The sizes and shapes of the bones in all these fossils tell a story. They tell scientists how and when birds began.

Ichthyornis

Before there were birds, there were reptiles. The earliest reptiles were very heavy creatures. They moved on four legs, like alligators, crocodiles, and most other reptiles that live today. They had thick, solid bones. Their legs were short, and their feet had five toes. These early reptiles mostly walked or crawled. Sometimes they ran for short distances, but they ran slowly.

Millions of years passed. New kinds of reptiles lived on the earth. Most of these reptiles were dinosaurs.

Not all the dinosaurs were big, heavy, and slow. The coelurosaurs (see-luro-saurs) were one kind of dinosaur. Their name means "hollow lizard." Coelurosaurs were small and light in weight. They stood on two legs and moved quickly. Scientists think one of this group of dinosaurs was the ancestor of Archaeopteryx.

Coelurosaur

Ornithosuchus

12

Ornithosuchus (Or-nitho-sookus) was a coelurosaur. Its name means "bird-crocodile." Ornithosuchus lived about two hundred million years ago. It was no bigger than a cat. It could run fast on its two feet. It caught animals and insects with its two hands. Each hand had only three fingers. Each foot had only four toes.

Some of Ornithosuchus's bones were hollow. They were very light. Ornithosuchus could move quickly. It could balance easily on two feet. It had large, strong muscles in its long, powerful legs.

At first, the reptile ancestors of birds used their front legs as arms. Then, over millions of years, the arms of the reptiles became the wings of the bird.

After Ornithosuchus, about sixty million years passed until the time of Archaeopteryx. During that time, other changes took place. One of the most important was the change from scales to feathers.

Reptiles have scales on their bodies. The coelurosaur ancestors of Archaeopteryx had scales. But as time passed, the scales changed. They became longer and lighter, with a thin shaft down the center. Millions of years passed. The ancestor that came just before Archaeopteryx had scales only on its head and feet. The rest of its body was covered with feathers.

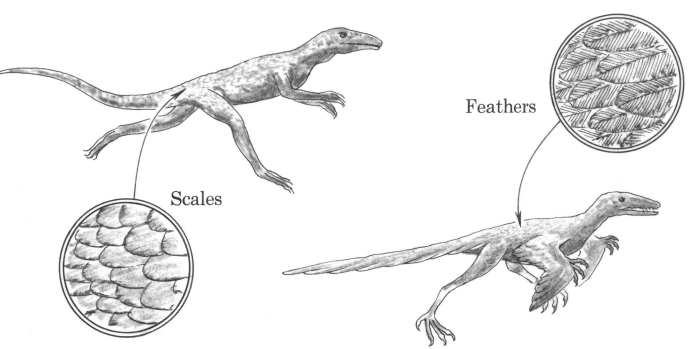

Feathers

Scales

Reptiles have no feathers. They are cold-blooded. Their bodies are as cold or as warm as the air around them. Lizards cool off so much at night they can hardly move. They must wait until the next day when it warms up again.

But when they get too hot, lizards cannot move either. In the hottest part of the day, they crawl into cool places. The bodies of the coelurosaurs cooled off and heated up in this same way.

Feathers Fluffed Up—
Body Heat Is Trapped

Feathers Open—
Body Heat Escapes

Once the bird ancestors had feathers, they did not cool off or overheat. If they got too cold, they fluffed up their feathers. This held warm air close to their bodies and kept them warm. If they got too hot, they opened up their feathers to let some heat escape. This kept them cool.

The ancestors that came just before Archaeopteryx were no longer reptiles. They were warm-blooded like the birds of today. Their bodies could keep working all the time.

Wing Feathers
of Archaeopteryx

At first, feathers grew only on the body and on parts of the arms and legs. But after millions of years, the feathers spread and became longer. They formed the wings and the tail. The feathers were large but very light.

Archaeopteryx had a much thinner skeleton than the earlier reptiles. Its skull was lighter. Its long tail was made mostly of feathers. Many of its bones were hollow and shaped like tubes. This gave the bones the greatest strength for the least weight. Archaeopteryx was light enough to fly.

Archaeopteryx

Scientists still don't know how birds first started to fly. The Archaeopteryx fossils give no answer to that question. But they do give some clues.

When a scientist tries to solve a problem, he often puts ideas and facts together to make a theory. Different scientists have different ideas, so there may be more than one theory about a problem.

There are two main theories about how birds began to fly. The first says that the ancestors of Archaeopteryx lived in trees. They jumped from branch to branch, hunting small animals and insects.

After millions of years, their bodies were feathered and warm-blooded. Feathers on their arms and tails became longer. When they jumped, these feathered parts helped to hold them up in the air. They could make long glides to chase and catch their prey.

By the time of Archaeopteryx, the arms had become even longer and stronger. They were like the wings of birds today. Now Archaeopteryx could glide from high places in the trees. It could catch insects in the air.

Sometimes the insects zoomed up to escape.
Archaeopteryx flapped its wings and tried to go
higher after them. But it could only fly for a few
moments. Once it had glided down to earth,
Archaeopteryx could not fly up again. It had to
use the claws on its wings and feet to climb back
up to a high place. Then it could glide down
again.

Gliding birds kept flapping and trying to lift themselves higher into the air. After millions of years, birds had larger wing muscles. They could lift themselves with their own wing power. They could fly high and far.

That is how some scientists think birds began to fly long ago. Other scientists think the ancestors of Archaeopteryx lived on the ground, not in trees. They think these creatures ran on two legs, hunting small animals and insects. In the beginning they caught insects by grabbing them with their jaws or their claws. But many insects escaped by darting away at the last moment.

After a long, long time, these bird ancestors
had a coat of feathers. Their arm and tail feathers
were long. They used their feathered arms to
catch insects.

They swatted insects to the ground.

They clapped their arms together
to trap insects in between.

They slapped insects and pushed them
into their mouths.

When they flapped their feathered arms in a certain way, they could lift themselves up from the ground. They could chase flying insects a short way upward and catch them in the air. Some scientists think this is how they started to use their arms as wings.

Did birds begin to fly by gliding down from trees or by flapping upward from the ground? No one knows yet which theory is right. Someday more clues may be discovered.

Someone may find a new fossil—one that lived between the time of the coelurosaurs and the time of Archaeopteryx. That might be the important clue. It might explain how the early birds first started to fly, millions of years ago.

ABOUT THE AUTHOR / ILLUSTRATOR

John Kaufmann has written and illustrated many books for children, several of which have dealt with different aspects of the principles of flight. His previous titles in the Let's-Read-and-Find-Out series are *Bats in the Dark* and *Streamlined*, and for older readers he has written *Robins Fly North, Robins Fly South.*

Mr. Kaufmann lives in Fresh Meadows, New York, with his wife, Alicia, and their two sons, Darius and Noel.